Copyright © 2019

Rainey Leigh Seraphine

Wizzenhill Publishing

All rights reserved. Without limiting the rights under copyright reserved above, no part of this work/publication may be reproduced, stored in or introduced into a retrieval system, or transmitted, in any form or by any means electronic, mechanical, print, photocopying, recording or otherwise), without the prior written permission of the copyright owner.

ISBN 978-0-6485458-8-0

For John and his little three legged dog, Piddling Pete!
He piddled on the ceiling
and he piddled on the floor
and when the butcher kicked him out
he piddled on the door!
John Gauld

For Helen and all the Gauld clan who would like to see
John's work as it should be,
a published book to treasure always.

It is an honour to work with this family!

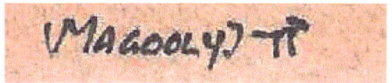

Look for Piddling Pete in some of the following pictures!

Australian Natives

in

Lilting Limerick

Volume 1

Emu

There once was an emu called Squirty,
who always looked scruffy and dirty!
His Mum had enough
of the dirt and the fluff,
kicked him out in the street
in the blistering heat
and cried don't you come back 'til you're thirty!
Poor Squirty!

"Emu." John. Gauld 18·4·19
(Magooly)

Greater Bilby and Bandy Bandy Snake

There once was a bilby called Bonny,
who suffered from wind in her belly.
When a slithering snake,
caused her body to shake,
and in terrible strife
with such fear for her life,
the wind blurted out of her bummy!
Poor Bonny!

Koala

There was a koala called Harry,
who wanted a female to marry.
He looked mighty fine,
and was terribly kind,
but the girl he adored,
was incessantly bored,
and ran off with his heart and his money!
Poor Harry!

Koala & Joey
24·6·19.

Crested Pigeon

There once was a pigeon called Penny,
who met a young pigeon called Benny,
she fluttered her lashes
with hopes of some pashes,
but Ben got a fright,
'cause he wanted no wife,
who would nag him to death in matrimony!
Poor Penny!

"Crested Pigeon"

John Gould 28·3·19
(Magooly)

Frill Necked Lizard

There once was a lizard called Izzy,
whose life was incredibly busy.
His frill was a mess
and caused terrible stress,
'cause way out of control,
his frill would unfold,
and he'd trip and he'd roll until dizzy!
Poor Izzy!

Frill necked Lizard.

Duckbill Platypus

There once was a platypus called Walter,
who was terribly scared of the water!
His mean friends would laugh,
as they watched from the path
and as Walter tried hard,
for his fears to discard,
he would get oh so close! And then falter!
Poor Walter!

"Duckbill Platypus." John. Gauld. 25·2·19
(Macool.)

Australian Magpie

There once was a magpie called Bob,
who believed it was always his job,
to dive-bomb the post man,
the kids and the milkman,
and threaten each head,
with his beak that would shred,
but the hard hats they wore made his head throb!
Poor Bob!

"Australian Magpie."

John Gauld. 10·3·19.
(Magooly.)

Feathertail Glider

There once was a glider called Sooky,
who tried oh so hard to be spooky!
She hid in the dark,
in the trees in the park
and threw gumnuts with glee
to make everyone flee,
then fell out of that tree! It was freaky!
Poor Sooky!

"Feathertail Glider." John Gould. 4-3-19. (Mardoly.)

Brahminy Kite

There once was a kite bird called Cecil,
who loved nothing more than to wrestle!
He drove his friends nuts,
with his hard headed butts,
and his mum lost her mind
when he grabbed her behind,
so she bushwhacked him out on the trestle!
Poor Cecil!

Green and Golden Bell Frog

There once was a bell frog called Jess,
who farted with flair and finesse!
But his wife had enough,
of his constant loud fluffs
and the smell that would seep,
made her eyes blink and weep,
so she left him in woeful distress!
Poor Jess!

"Green & Golden Bell Frogs".
TOP - FEMALE — BTM. - MALE.

John. Gauld. 12·6·19.
(Magooly.)

Eastern Rosella

There was a rosella called Bella,
who was loved by a quite handsome fella!
She liked how he looked,
as his beak nicely hooked
and his feathers were bright
looking flashy in flight,
but he was thick as a brick and no pleasure!
Poor Bella!

Eastern Rosella
22·6·19.

Kangaroo

Hugh was a huge kangaroo,
who boxed every bloke in his crew!
They each had enough,
grabbed his neck by the scruff,
pinned him down to the ground,
getting ready to pound,
and then realised they'd pinned him in poo!
Poor Hugh!

Kangaroo.
23.6.19.

The Getting of a Lairdship
(Like the Getting of Wisdom, but really nothing like it!)
by John Gauld
18 March 2015 (the day after St Patrick's Day)

Reidy's going off, like a frog in a sock
cos he thinks he's the Laird of a place called Black Rock.
He claims to be of Scottish descent,
proudly this is true, so there is no lament,
so for him to make this lofty ascent,
proof is required that he's not too bent.

Scotland is known as the land of the free
they're not all perfect, you must agree,
so Reidy being not a 100 percent,
fits the criteria being not too bent.

The Lord Chancellor of all the jocks,
summoned 'The Reid' to the starting blocks,
"Laddie," he said, "you're not yet a Laird,
a title like this is not easily snared.
There's criteria to be met, this is not a scam,
to be Laird ye have to drink a wee dram."

The Reid's eyes lit up, this was right up his alley,
"Give me the drink and keep the tally
and I'll show you Scots, I can certainly swally."
So off 'the Reid' went and had the odd one or twenty,
Lord Chancellor impressed, said "You've had plenty."
"Sir Ronald," he said, "You have passed the test,
tho' a bit too willing in demonstrating your best."

"I dub thee Sir Ronald the Laird of Black Rock,
the bloodline is there, you're of good Scottish stock.
So back to Australia, you look pretty puffed,
and tell that Magooly to go and get stuffed!"

Yee Ha!
Kind Regards,
Laird Mucken Fagooly

Other books by Rainey Leigh Seraphine for children:

We're Off to the Moon in My Hot Air Balloon
Miranda Merbaby's Mystical World
Wicky the Wacky Witch & Grumpy Mr Whilloby
Bronte's Book
Our Dad Hates Bugs
The Snowflake Who Wouldn't Fall
Where is the Easter Bunny
The Fairies Tale
Aristotle The Rebel
Theo's World (about Dwarfism)
Skiddy Squirrel's Poetically Preposterous Account of
Awesome Animal Antics
Greta's Dilemma
The Pappinbarra Flood
Bonny Bilby
Australian Natives in Lilting Limerick Volume 2

Available at all online bookstores and retail outlets.

Visit: www.raineyleighseraphine.com
or author's Facebook page: raineyleighseraphine

www.ingramcontent.com/pod-product-compliance
Lightning Source LLC
Chambersburg PA
CBHW042144290426
44110CB00002B/103